Get Well Soon

SPIRITUAL LIGHT PUBLISHING

NAME:

_____

WISHES:

_____

_____

_____

_____

_____

_____

_____

NAME:

_____

WISHES:

_____

_____

_____

_____

_____

_____

_____

NAME:

_____

WISHES:

_____

_____

_____

_____

_____

_____

_____

NAME:

_____

WISHES:

_____

_____

_____

_____

_____

_____

_____

NAME:

_____

WISHES:

_____

_____

_____

_____

_____

_____

_____

NAME:

_____

WISHES:

_____

_____

_____

_____

_____

_____

_____

NAME:

_____

WISHES:

_____

_____

_____

_____

_____

_____

NAME:

_____

WISHES:

_____

_____

_____

_____

_____

_____

NAME:

_____

WISHES:

_____

_____

_____

_____

_____

_____

NAME:

WISHES:

NAME:

_____

WISHES:

_____

_____

_____

_____

_____

_____

_____

NAME:

_____

WISHES:

_____

_____

_____

_____

_____

_____

NAME:

_____

WISHES:

_____

_____

_____

_____

_____

_____

_____

NAME:

_____

WISHES:

_____

_____

_____

_____

_____

_____

NAME:

_____

WISHES:

_____

_____

_____

_____

_____

_____

_____

NAME:

_____

WISHES:

_____

_____

_____

_____

_____

_____

NAME:

_____

WISHES:

_____

_____

_____

_____

_____

_____

_____

NAME:

WISHES:

_____

_____

_____

_____

_____

_____

_____

NAME:

_____

WISHES:

_____

_____

_____

_____

_____

_____

_____

NAME:

_____

WISHES:

_____

_____

_____

_____

_____

_____

NAME:

WISHES:

NAME:

_____

WISHES:

_____

_____

_____

_____

_____

_____

NAME:

_____

WISHES:

_____

_____

_____

_____

_____

_____

_____

NAME:

_____

WISHES:

_____

_____

_____

_____

_____

_____

NAME:

_____

WISHES:

_____

_____

_____

_____

_____

_____

_____

NAME:

_____

WISHES:

_____

_____

_____

_____

_____

_____

_____

NAME:

_____

WISHES:

_____

_____

_____

_____

_____

_____

NAME:

_____

WISHES:

_____

_____

_____

_____

_____

_____

_____

NAME:

_____

WISHES:

_____

_____

_____

_____

_____

_____

_____

NAME:

_____

WISHES:

_____

_____

_____

_____

_____

_____

_____

NAME:

_____

WISHES:

_____

_____

_____

_____

_____

_____

_____

NAME:

_____

WISHES:

_____

_____

_____

_____

_____

_____

_____

NAME:

_____

WISHES:

_____

_____

_____

_____

_____

_____

_____

NAME:

_____

WISHES:

_____

_____

_____

_____

_____

_____

_____

NAME:

_____

WISHES:

_____

_____

_____

_____

_____

_____

_____

NAME:

_____

WISHES:

_____

_____

_____

_____

_____

_____

_____

NAME:

_____

WISHES:

_____

_____

_____

_____

_____

_____

NAME:

_____

WISHES:

_____

_____

_____

_____

_____

_____

_____

NAME:

_____

WISHES:

_____

_____

_____

_____

_____

_____

_____

NAME:

_____

WISHES:

_____

_____

_____

_____

_____

_____

NAME:

_____

WISHES:

_____

_____

_____

_____

_____

_____

_____

NAME:

_____

WISHES:

_____

_____

_____

_____

_____

_____

_____

NAME:

WISHES:

NAME:

_____

WISHES:

_____

_____

_____

_____

_____

_____

_____

NAME:

_____

WISHES:

_____

_____

_____

_____

_____

_____

_____

NAME:

_____

WISHES:

_____

_____

_____

_____

_____

_____

_____

NAME:

_____

WISHES:

_____

_____

_____

_____

_____

_____

_____

NAME:

_____

WISHES:

_____

_____

_____

_____

_____

_____

_____

NAME:

WISHES:

NAME:

WISHES:

Made in the USA
Middletown, DE
20 December 2024